Jokes You Shouldn't Tell A Dog!

by Eric Arnold

D1475795

Aladdin Paperbacks

To the memory of Ben Solomon—
A perfect soul with a wonderful spirit and smile!
"Hat's on!"—always to Adam and Rochelle
For Tali and Gabe—my ray of sunshine each and every day!
Thank you to Vivien Cohen, Teacher Extraordinaire,
and to Judy Botsford, Librarian Extraordinaire, and to
the entire Runkle School community!

A very special thanks to my
editor and friend, Steve Fraser!

First Aladdin Paperbacks edition September 1999

Text copyright © 1999 by Eric Arnold
Illustrations copyright © 1999 by Sean Taggart

Aladdin Paperbacks
An imprint of Simon & Schuster Children's Publishing Division
1230 Avenue of the Americas
New York, NY 10020

Designed by Steve Scott
The text for this book is set in Caecilia.
The illustrations were rendered in pen and ink.
Printed and bound in the United States of America
2 4 6 8 10 9 7 5 3 1

Library of Congress Catalog Card Number: 99-64238
ISBN 0-689-83094-7 (pbk.)

Jokes You Shouldn't Tell A Dog!

The Computer Dog!

Juan: Why is it hard for Chihuahuas to type on a keyboard?
Justin: They're all paws.

Alexa: How are you going to pay the Chihuahua who helped you to set up your computer?
Polly: With dog diskettes!

Basset Hound: What kind of computer do you want to buy?
Chihuahua: One with a small byte!

Sarah: What kind of computers do chihuahuas like best?
Chihuahua: Lap-top!

The Sports Dog!

Sarah: What does a Chihuahua play basketball with?
Janaina: A tennis ball!

From the "Good Things Come in Small Packages" department: Chihuahuas are the smallest breed of dog in the world! They weigh less than 2 1/4 pounds (1 kilogram). The largest Chihuahua can tip the scales at about 4 1/2 pounds (2 kilograms)—whew!

Catherine: Why did the Chihuahua take the bus to the TV studio to make a commercial?
Abbie: It was too far to walk!

Luisa: What does a Chihuahua wear to play basketball?
Shakti: Small basketball shoes!

What do you get when you cross a poodle and a pointer? Why a "pudelpointer," of course! This is an actual dog, which was developed in Germany to "work" as a sporting dog, good at retrieving, tracking, and pointing!

Tali: Why couldn't the Chihuahua play basketball?
Gabe: Because its basketball shoes were in the wash and a tennis player needed the ball!

What do you think the fastest dog is? If you said a dog being chased by another dog, you're half right! It's a toss-up between the greyhound, which can reach a speed of 37 mph (60kmh) and the azawaka and the whippet, which have been clocked at speeds up to 40 mph (64 kmh)!

Ben: What has twelve legs and runs but can hardly be seen?
Adam: A bulldog on a jog in the fog with its friends, the hog and the frog.

Koby: What is the only breed of dog a boxer is afraid of?
Jared: A Doberman puncher!

Boston Terrier: Was your master playing catch with you?
Chihuahua: No, I was playing throw with her!

Kazu: What dog would you want on your football team?
Ariel: A golden receiver!

Emma: What is a Chihuahua's favorite sport?
Zac: Miniature golf!

Rebecca: What position is the best for a Chihuahua to play in baseball?
Carlos: Shortstop!

Jake: Do you like this dog over here?
Meg: No, I like the otter hound!

Some breeds of hound dogs were developed to hunt a certain animal. Bloodhounds, for example, were first developed to track boars. Some of these hounds take their names from the kinds of animals they were trained to hunt. For example, the otter hound was developed in England to hunt otters, and the foxhound was developed to hunt, well, you know, foxes!

Melanie: Why can't Chihuahuas run marathons?
Fred: They're short of breath!

Jennifer: What has eighteen legs and fetches a ball?
James: The Philadelphia Beagles!

Emily: How do you know which Chihuahua can ride a bike?
Timeka: It's the one wearing a helmet!

Zack: What kind of bugs bother sporting dogs?
Jeremy: Ath-fleats!

Nicole: How can you make a basset hound fast?
Allie: Take away its food!

Tom: Can your dog catch a ball?
Pedro: My dog couldn't catch a cold!

Here's an amazing flea fact! The flea that is no friend to a dog is also quite an athlete itself! Its hind legs are huge and it can "jump" 8 inches (20 centimeters) high and 13 inches (33 centimeters) across. If that doesn't sound like a lot, think of it this way: If a person had the same leaping ability as a flea, he or she could jump 1,000 feet (2,540 centimeters) straight up! NBA—are you listening?

Carlos: How come a flea can jump so high?
Kendra: It's got amazing fleat!

Did you ever wonder why fleas are so musical in Hawaii? Well, you know that tiny guitar called a "ukulele?" The word ukulele is Hawaiian for "little jumping flea!" That's got to be music to somebody's ears!

The Shopping Dog!

Matthew: What kind of leash should you buy for a Chihuahua?
Jenna: A short one!

Ian: Where will a springer spaniel never shop?
Sayo: At a flea market!

From the "Fleeting News" department: How fast can a flea flee? Pretty quickly! In fact, a flea can "accelerate," or get up to speed, fifty times faster than the space shuttle! But why would a flea be in such a big hurry, anyway? Where does it really have to go?

The Show Business Dog!

A Chihuahua was shopping in a mall when another shopper walked up to it and started talking.

Shopper: Didn't I see you on a TV commercial?

Chihuahua: How am I supposed to know what you watch on TV?

Here's a two-part question: What was the name of Dorothy's dog in the movie The Wizard of Oz, and what kind of dog was he?
(answer below)

Karen: Where did the Chihuahua sign its contract for its TV commercials?

Maria: On the bottom!

The dog's name was Toto and it was a cairn terrier (but in L. Frank Baum's book, The Wonderful Wizard of Oz, from which the movie was made, Toto was a Boston terrier!)

9

*Here's a hard one: In Peter Pan by J. M. Barrie,
the nursemaid to the Darling children is actually
a dog. What was the dog's name and
what kind of dog was it?
(answer below)*

Van: Do Chihuahuas have horns?
Ryan: Many have violins but very few have horns!

From the "What a Pal!" department: Lots of movies and TV shows were first based on books. For example, before Lassie, the collie, became known as a movie and TV star, she was the heroine in the book, Lassie Come Home. When a movie company in Hollywood decided to make a movie of the book, three hundred dogs were auditioned before a dog named Pal was given the part—even though Pal was a male dog! In fact, in all of the Lassie movies and the long-running TV series, all of the dogs who eventually played Lassie were males!

The dog was a Newfoundland and its name was Nana. J. M. Barrie's own dog, Luath, was the inspiration for the character of Nana.

Amrita: Why should you never watch a video with a Chihuahua?
Jeremy: It always plays with the "paws" button on the VCR.

Who was Beethoven? (Two possible answers for this question—one furry and one not!)
(answer below)

Can you name at least five movies (animation included) that feature a dog in a main role?
—Were you able to do it? Here's a list of some well-known "dog movies": Air Bud, Air Retriever, 101 Dalmations, Oh! Heavenly Dog, Napoleon, The Shaggy Dog, Old Yeller, Lady and the Tramp, Benji, Lassie Come Home, Beethoven, Annie *(Sandy the dog)*, Balto, Peter Pan *(Nana the nurse-maiden)*, Shiloh, The Incredible Journey, The Littlest Hobo, Milo and Otis, The Shaggy Dog, *and Wizard of Oz. Can you name others?*

1. Beethoven was the film name of the Saint Bernard who starred in the movie of of the same name, Beethoven. The Saint Bernard who played Beethoven in the movie had the real name of Chris. 2. The human, Ludwig von Beethoven (1770–1827), was a famous German composer. Da, da, da, dum. Da, da, da, dum . . .

11

From the "You Ought to Be in Movies" department: If you know of a dog that you think has some acting talent, there is a "doggie college" in Los Angeles that offers an eight-week acting course for dogs! Can law school or medical school for dogs be far behind?

You might have seen the old or new Little Rascals movies. Pretty funny, weren't they? Remember the dog with the circle around its eye?
What was the dog's name?
(answer below)

Pete. By the way, the circle was drawn on the dog just for the movie. In some Little Rascals movies, the circle appears around the right eye and in other movies, it appears around the left eye!

12

The International Dog!

Bridget: How do you say "Chihuahua" in Spanish?
Ava: Chihuahua.

What dog would Dracula like as a pet?
(answer below)

Isabel: How does a poodle say hello in France?
Sophie: Bone-jour!

Would you name a dog after a butterfly? Well, if it had ears that looked like a butterfly, maybe you would! The papillon is named after a butterfly because that's how you say "butterfly" in French!

A Transylvanian hound—this is a real dog that was originally used to hunt wolves and bears!

Michael: What do you call an injured dog leaving town for Madrid?
Brenna: A Great Dane with a cane on its way to a plane to get to Spain!

From the "Interplanetary Cartoon-Dog" department: Did you ever see the classic cartoon series, or the movie, The Jetsons? Well, the Jetsons had a family dog. Do you remember what this outer space dog that looked a bit like a Great Dane was named?
(answer "A" below)

Tristan: What is a favorite vacation spot for Chihuahuas?
Susan: Boneos Aires, Argentina!

David: What dog is always tired in London?
Aaron: An English sleep dog.

Okay, if a breed of dog began in Italy and it looked like a fox, what would you call this breed?
(see answer "B" below)

Mia: How do you say "Chihuahua" in Italy?
Maya: Chihuahua!

A: Astro   B: Volpino, because volpe means a fox in Italian!

Julia: What does a French poodle say before each meal?
Will: Bone appetit!

Jesse: What is brown and gray, has eight legs, and is carrying a large trunk and a small trunk?
Anna: A Chihuahua on vacation with an elephant.

The Well-Dressed Dog!

Sally: What do you get when you cross a Chihuahua with an English sheepdog?
Amy: Small wool sweaters!

Speaking of sweaters, did you know that some humans knit sweaters made out of dog hair? Not that sheep and their wool are going to be put out of business, but dog hair sweaters are becoming a bit trendy! Knitters prefer using the hair of longhair dogs like collies, and the hair of a golden retriever is also very popular. How does dog hair compare with wool? Well, folks who knit dog hair think it's better because it doesn't shrink, it's very warm, and it's not as "ruff" as wool (it really is supposed to be smoother than wool!—no kidding)!

Karina: What kind of dog is the most colorful?
Meredith: A paint Bernard!

Dima: What is black and white and red all over?

Joanna: A Chihuahua in a tuxedo that tripped into a jar of salsa!

From the "This Is a Hard One!" department: Do you remember the classic children's book, Eloise? It was about a girl who lived in New York City in the Plaza Hotel. Well, aside from Eloise's turtle, Skipperdee, she also had a rather unusual dog that wore sunglasses and actually looked more like a cat.
Do you remember what the dog's name was?
(answer below)

Eliza: What kind of pants do you buy for your pet Chihuahua?

Suman: Shorts!

Eliza: And what kind of socks should you buy?

Suman: Anklets!

Nathan: What wears a black, white, and tan coat but has no hair?

Raphael: A bald beagle!

What do you think is the tallest breed of dog?
(answer below)

Alejandra: Why was the Alaskan malamute wearing suspenders?
Christen: To hold up its snow pants!

The Well-Groomed Dog!

Manny: What kind of dog always needs a shave?
Ari: A bearded collie!

The basenji, also known as a Congo terrier or Congo dog, cleans itself with its tongue like a feline. And, when it runs, it has the same type of gait as a thoroughbred horse.

Melissa: What side of a Chihuahua has the most hair?
Hanna: The outside!

Isaiah: When do Chihuahuas smell?
Jake: When they don't take a bath!

Ashley: How do Chihuahuas smell?
Elena: With their nose!

Avi: What do you call a bunch of bugs that bother a dog?
Tali: A fleat!

Ashley: What happened to the French poodle's new haircut when it rained?
Imer: It got wet!

From the "Head to Tail" department: There's probably not a dog better prepared for getting wet than the Portuguese water dog. Its tail even has a special tuft of hair on it so it will float when the dog is swimming!

Greyhound: How did you find the fleas?
Beagle: I didn't! They found me!

From the "A Face Only a Mother (or Father) Could Love" department: If you could magnify a flea a thousand times, it looks like a lobster! Its head is mostly a beak, so it is pretty good at piercing things—ouch!

The Super Dog!

Isaac: What wears a cape, flies through the air, and wears a mask with pointy ears?
Celia: Super-Chihuahua that borrowed Batman's mask!

*What do you call a "superdog" that wore a cape
in a classic cartoon series?*
(answer "A" below)

*And, what do you call the "Superdog" that is
an occasional companion of Superman?*
(answer "B" below)

A: Why, "Underdog," of course, of the classic cartoon series, which bears his name! Let's hope that Underdog and Polly Purebred will, one day, find true happiness together.   B: Krypto

The Well-Taken Care of Dog!

Brandon: What do you do when a Chihuahua sneezes?
Adrianne: Get a small hankie!

Jared: Where do you take a Chihuahua that has fallen into a lake?
Katya: To a weterinarian!

Gabriel: Have you checked your German shepherd's eyes lately?
Malik: Why? They've always been brown!

Suman: My friend only believes in having purebred dogs as pets.
Diego: Why? As long as your pet is a good dog and you love it, it doesn't really mutter what kind it is!

Diwali: How do you take a Chihuahua's temperature?
Alice: With a small thermometer!

White House Dogs and Their Presidents

Buddy, a black Lab —Bill Clinton

Millie, an English springer spaniel —George Bush

Lucky, a sheepdog —Ronald Reagan

Him and Her, two beagles; Yuki, a mutt
    —Lyndon Johnson

Timahoe, an Irish setter —Richard Nixon

Clipper, a German shepherd —John F. Kennedy

Mike, an Irish setter —Harry Truman

Heidi, a weimaraner —Dwight Eisenhower

Fala, a Scottie; Major, a German shepherd
    —Franklin Roosevelt

King Tut, a German shepherd —Herbert Hoover

Laddie Boy, an Airedale; Oh Boy, an English bulldog
    —Warren G. Harding

Rob Roy, a white collie —Calvin Coolidge

Skip, a mutt —Theodore Roosevelt

Grim, a brindle greyhound —Rutherford B. Hayes

Faithful, a Newfoundland —Ulysses S. Grant

Elyssa: What's the best way to measure a Chihuahua?
Sasha: With a ruler!

From the "Dogs Fit for a Queen" department: The Queen Victoria had over a hundred dogs! She certainly must have liked purebred dogs. For example, she had six Pomeranians—Beppo, Fluffy, Gilda, Lula, Mino, and Nino. It seems that she had fun naming them too! It was the queen who actually helped to popularize the Pomeranian breed. She also had a black Lab named Sharp and a dachshund named Deckel. It's a good thing she had a lot of space for kennels at Windsor Castle!

The Hungry Dog!

Beth: How did your Chihuahua break its leg?
Emma: I dropped some dog food on it by accident.

Beth: But that couldn't have broken its leg.
Emma: The dog food was still in the can!

Here's a hard one: On the front of the Cracker Jack box, there is a picture of a boy with his black-and-white dog. What is the name of the dog and, for extra credit, what is the name of the boy?
(answer below)

Whitney: How do Chihuahuas eat so much?
Daniel: They make a lot go a little way!

Jessica: Why did the Chihuahua ask the bloodhound to take it to a restaurant?
David: Because the bloodhound just found a lot of scents!

The dog's name is Bingo and the boy's name is "Jack the Sailor Boy." By the way, Bingo's been on the Cracker Jack box since 1919!

Mary: Why was the beagle only eating canned dog food?
Oliver: Because it didn't pay its bone bill!

Rebecca: What dog sweats the most and drinks the most water?
Daria: A hot-weiler!

Basset Hound: I was thinking of inviting my friend, the beagle, over for breakfast.
What do you think I should serve?
Chihuahua: That's easy! Beagles and cream cheese go great together!

From the "Fleacula" department: Every day, a female flea drinks fifteen times her body weight in blood!

Max: What is your dog's favorite breakfast?
Ross: Pooched eggs!

Audrey: How can you tell if a Chihuahua has been in the refrigerator?
Abigail: Paw prints in the butter!

Ben: What should you do if you have a basset hound over for dinner?
Adam: Have a short table!

Rachel: What did the Labrador retriever say to its bone?
Celia: It was nice gnawing you!

Anthony: What dog is always hungry?
Taylor: A Chow Chow!

The Fun Dog!

Ramon: What do you call a boring dog?
Samuel: A dull-mation!

Ethan: What do you call a dizzy dog at an amusement park?
Honoka: A bloodhound on the ground not making a sound after riding a fast merry-go-round!

What was the name of the Muppet dog who
performed very unfunny comedy routines?
(answer "A" below)

Anna: What do you call a dog in a hurry that falls in a puddle on the way to the post office?
Andrew: An Irish setter that is a go-getter that got wetter while mailing a letter!

In the Peanuts comic strip,
what kind of dog is Snoopy?
(answer "B" below)

A: Rowlf   B: A beagle

Lily: What is a beagle's favorite board game?
Charlotte: Boneopoly!

Here's a harder "Snoopy" question:
Where was Snoopy born?
(answer "A" below)

Golden Retriever: What is your favorite holiday?
Chihuahua: Howloween!

Springer Spaniel: Why do you like to go on camping trips?
Chihuahua: I like to "ruff" it!

If you have ever read Dennis the Menace comics or seen the movies, you might know the answer to this rough question: What was the name of Dennis's dog?
(answer "B" below)

One of the cartoon world's funniest dogs is Goofy, from the Disney Studios. But, did you know what his original name was before it was changed to Goofy?
(answer "C" below)

A: Daisy Hill Puppy Farm   B: Ruff   C: He was first created as "Dippy Dawg," when he appeared in Mickey's Review in 1932. His name was later changed to Googy in 1939. But, no matter what he was called, like all dogs, he never wanted to be called late to dinner.

The Smart Dog!

Leslie: What dog wears a white coat and does science experiments?
Tricia: Labs!

Do you think Dr. Doolittle expected the "ruff language" he heard from his dog, Jip? Jip was the first dog to be able to communicate with the doctor in the classic book, Dr. Doolittle, by Hugh Lofting.

Nathaniel: What is the best kind of dog to ask for directions?
Kiara: A Chihuahua, because it knows all the shortcuts!

Cecilia: How can you tell a dogwood tree?
Nora: By its bark!

The smartest cartoon dog has to be Professor Peabody who appeared on the classic cartoon series, The Rocky and Bullwinkle Show. In fact, Professor Peabody had his own "boy," much like a human has a pet dog. He would send his boy, Sherman, on great adventures through his time machine.

Adam: How do you spell "Chihuahua?"
Ben: "C-h-i-w-o-w-a."
Adam: That's not even close!
Ben: But you asked me how I spelled it!

Lisa: What kind of dog is the smartest?
Diego: A great brain!

The cartoon world has a classic cartoon series that features a Great Dane. What was the name of the dog, which is also the name of the series?
(answer below)

Jason: What dog can beat a spelling bee?
Cal: A cocker spaniel that can spell "bell" or "sell" but also "gazelle," "parallel," and even "mademoiselle!"

Boston terriers must not think people are very smart, because whoever named this breed made a huge mistake. A Boston terrier was, indeed, developed in Boston, but it isn't a terrier. It is more bulldog than terrier!

Liana: What kind of dog can tell time?
Patti: A clockshund!

Natalie: Why does a Chihuahua have four legs?
Jennifer: So it can count past three!

Thomas: Every time I tell my English Setter to stop barking, it never does!

Carlos: What does it do?

Thomas: It just stands on its back two legs and quotes Shakespeare!

Carlos: What?

Thomas: Yeah, it says, "To bark or not to bark—that is the question!" and keeps on barking!

The Artistic Dog!

Collie: What did you do in art class today?
Chihuahua: Panting on paper!

Benjamin: What do you call a dog that was shopping for pasta but stopped to draw, instead?
Malik: A poodle who was looking to buy a noodle but decided to doodle.

Amy: What artistic dog chews a lot and follows the rules of the farm where it lives?
Joseph: A Chihuahua that can draw and gnaw while obeying the law and lying on straw!

Steven: What kind of modeling clay does a dog use?
Manuel: Fi-Do!

Melanie: Mom, I just spotted a Chihuahua!
Mom: Melanie, that wasn't very nice!

From the "Don't be Shocked" department: A litter of Dalmation puppies can be pretty large—usually six to eight puppies. These adorable puppies, however, are born all white, without any spots or markings. It's not until after the second week that spots begin to appear. All of the markings are fully developed after the dog is about one year old—so mark your calendar!

Jamal: Dad, I spotted a Dalmatian!
Dad: No need to, son, it already has its own spots!

The Working Dog!

Camila: What kind of dogs are the best with children?
Wendy: Baby setters!

Why are Dalmations known as "firehouse dogs?" Before fire trucks were engine-powered trucks, they were actually horse-drawn wagons. The Dalmation was known to be comfortable around horses, and it became a trusty companion in firehouses during the horse-powered fire wagon days. Dalmations also gained reputations as excellent watch dogs. If you see a Dalmation in a firehouse today, its job today is to be a faithful companion and pet to the firefighters in the firehouse.

Maria: What do you get when you cross a sled dog with an elephant?
Suzanne: A tusky!

Daniel: What is purple, blows a whistle, and sits in a high chair?
Carlos: A Saint Bernard working hard as a lifeguard wearing a leotard!

In American history, explorers Lewis and Clark set out in 1804 to search for the Northwest Passage—a water route to the Pacific Ocean. Traveling with them was Seaman, Lewis's black Newfoundland. Seaman was also a hero when bison charged Lewis and others in their camp in Montana. Seaman pushed the men out of the way and chased the bison away!

Tali: When George Washington was a general, why did he like to have dogs around?
Gabe: They were very helpful during the "Roverlutionary War!"

Irene: What is the best kind of dog to direct traffic at a busy intersection?
Samantha: A pointer!

The Musical Dog!

Paul: What dog has an excellent memory for music?
Ceci: A whippet is a pet that will never forget how to play a duet on a clarinet!

It's a known fact that dogs can hear better than people but how much better? Can a dog hear sounds two times farther away than a person can? Or, is it three times, four times, or five? What do you think? A dog can hear sounds four times farther away than a human can. So, if you don't want a dog to hear you talking about it, you better speak very softly and very far away!

Deborah: You see all of those dogs standing in line for the concert?
Cal: Yup!
Deborah: Well, why are they all scratching so much?
Cal: Oh, that's the line for all of the dogs who have tickets!

Sarah: What do you get when you mix a collie with a trumpet?
Andy: A Lassie who plays brassie!

Kathleen: Why did the Chihuahua bark when it heard a song on the radio?
Rami: It didn't know the words!

Way back in the dark ages, 1956 to be exact, singer Elvis Presley had a huge hit with his record, "Hound Dog." But, in 1965, the group called the Singing Dogs had a huge hit with "Jingle Bells."

Beagle: Where do you go to practice your singing?
Chihuahua: The barking lot!

If you're ever thinking of going to a concert to hear a dog sing, be sure the dog is a New Guinea Singing Dog. Yup, that's the full name of this breed. This dog's howl has a very unique sound—it sounds like a very sad song being sung!

Karim: If a beagle can't play a bugle in the marching band, what's his other favorite instrument to play?
Robert: A trombone.

From the "Its Howl Is Worse Than Its Bite" department: What does the bark of a basenji sound like? —First of all, a basenji rarely barks! It does, however, have a howling good time because it likes to howl. But, its howl sounds more like a yodel or a chortle!

The Family Dog!

Evan: What dog is a cousin to the Dalmatian?
Erica: A spot-weiler!

Melissa: Why are Chihuahuas such good bedtime storytellers?
Lauren: They have short tales!

Ever wonder how the name "Rover" became such a popular name for a dog? It was none other than George Washington, himself, who named one of his hunting dogs "Rover" and the name, you could say, really caught on.

Kevin: What kind of dog is very scary on Halloween?
Ramon: A ghouldog!

To say that George Washington liked dogs is an understatement! Besides Rover, he had dogs that he named Sweetlips, Truelove, and Venus. You can tell how much he liked these dogs by the affectionate names he gave them. He had other dogs, to name a few, named Vulcan, Busy, Taster, Forester, Mopsy, and Searcher. He sure needed a lot of dog food!

Alexandra: What dog lives in a small house surrounded by holes in the ground?
Jill: A mutt that lives in a hut near where people putt!

The family dog is faithful to its master—most of the time, hopefully! That's how the name "Fido" became popular for dogs. You see, the name "Fido" is short for the Latin word fidelis which means "faithful." Abe Lincoln had a dog named Fido before he became president. By the way, the Latin word fidelis also applies to the motto of the U.S. Marine Corps: Semper Fidelis—Always Faithful.

Charlotte: What does a Chihuahua call its mom and dad?
Julia: Chimama and Chipapa!

Paul Bunyan, the bigger-than-life mythical lumberjack, had a faithful companion, Babe, the Blue Ox. But, do you know the name of his dog?
(answer below)

Snookuns. Find out more about this dog on page 50.

The Happy and Friendly Dog!

Alex: What dog do other dogs tell their problems to?
Jordan: A complaint Bernard!

Megan: What dog is a friend to cozy insects?
Andrae: A pug giving a warm tug and a hug to a bug that's snug in a rug!

Tristan: What talks a lot, has fourteen legs, and speeds through traffic?
Adam: A blabbing Lab and a crab sharing a cab!

Joseph: What kind of dog is a person's best friend?
Amy: A palmatian!

Katherine: What is a collie puppy's favorite toy?
Caleb: A chew-chew train!

The Annoying Dog!

Jonathan: What dog takes the money and runs—fast!
Jake: A payhound!

Liz: What dog always gets on everyone's nerves?
Chloe: A great pane!

Zac: Why is everything in your home damaged?
Beth: My dog is in the middle of being housebroken!

Luisa: When are Pomeranians good at taking photographs?
Carl: Only when they snap at something!

German Shepherd: I'll see you shortly.
Chihuahua: Okay, but don't call me "Shortly!"

What dog wouldn't mind a trip to the South Pole? Well, certainly not a dachshund—get it (hot dog/weiner dog!)? Admiral Richard Byrd took his fox terrier along for his flight over the South Pole. The dog, unfortunately, was not the best travel companion under these harsh conditions and Admiral Byrd regretted taking his dog along. What do you think the dog's name was? (answer below)

Cassie: What was the most vicious and meanest dinosaur of them all?
Jamie: The Chihuahuasaurus Rex!

Igloo

The Helpful Dog!

Gilberto: What dog do other dogs go to when they are sick?
Aliza: A docs-hund!

Great Dane: How come you are always so well behaved when you go on a walk with your master?
Chihuahua: It's the leash I can do!

The Tricky Dog!

Nina: How does a Chihuahua hide in the desert?
Lara: It uses camel-flage!

Louisa: How did the Chihuahua disappear on the road?
Adriana: It was using a hide-'n-go-seekle!

David: What do you call a bug that bothers dogs on Halloween?
Ricky: A trick-or-fleat!

The Unusual Dog Breed!

Isaac: What is green, barks, and carries a torch?
Noah: The statue of Chihuahua!

You would probably think the "official national dog" of Ireland would be green, right? Well, it's actually blue—the Kerry blue terrier! It's born black, but its coat changes to blue between nine and twenty-four months of age.

Maya: What dog rides a horse named Macaroni?
Kaylie: Yankee poodle!

Anya: What kind of dog doesn't do well in hot weather?
Katoya: A faint Bernard!

What do you get when you cross a dachshund with a wolfhound? You get "Snookuns," Paul Bunyan's dog. Its tall wolfhound legs were in the back and its short dachshund legs were in the front—perfect for speeding downhill!

Janice: What do you get when you cross a bull-dog with a sheepdog?
Carol: A wooldog that shrinks when wet!

Pluto, the Disney dog, was an unusual breed for a cartoon dog. He didn't talk even though the mouse that owned him—Mickey Mouse—did. Pluto made his screen debut in Mickey's Pal Pluto in 1933.

Ben: What do you get when you cross a Chihuahua with a brave giraffe?
Adam: A Chihuahua that is not afraid to stick its neck out!

What do you get when you cross
a Labrador retriever and a poodle?
(answer below)

A labradoodle! This is a real breed of dog, which is pretty new. It's only been developed since 1989. The purpose of this new breed has been to develop a seeing eye dog for blind people who are allergic to dog fur because standard poodles don't shed!

Richie: What do you get when you cross a Doberman with a bird?
Kevin: A Doberman fincher!

The Watch Dog!

Katie: Why didn't the German shepherd bark when the robber broke into the house?
Nasim: It had laryngitis!

If you think that someone with the nickname of "Wart" might have a hard time finding suitable names for his dogs, think again. First, it was none other than King Arthur, himself (in the classic The Sword in the Stone by T. H. White), who had the nickname of "Wart" in his youth, and he had around eighteen dogs with such decent, and some very interesting, dog names as Lion, Bounce, Bungey, Toby, Diamond, Gerland, Luffra, Trowneer, Bran, Gerlert, and Clumsy. It's anyone's guess whether young Arthur needed these dogs as watchdogs once he acquired his not-so-flattering nickname.

Elizabeth: What kind of dog can you best see in the dark?
Farisa: A glowberman pinscher!

Koby: What kind of dog only comes out at night?
Ricky: A dusky husky!

The Lost Dog!

Dalia: What do you say to a Chihuahua that is running away?
Emily: Adios!

Gabe: What is the best way to follow a lost dog's paw prints?
Kei: With a track-tor!

Simone: How do you know if a dog is lost?
Robby: When it's barking up the wrong tree?

Becky: What dogs never get lost?
Brett: Newfound-lands!

The Dog Who Has a Silly Owner!

Zachary: What do Chihuahuas have that no other dogs have?
Margaret: Baby Chihuahuas!

Denzil: Why was the Chihuahua glad it wasn't an eagle?
Patricia: It can't fly!

From the "Okay, Who Named This Dog Breed?" department: We hope that the "Danish chicken dog" never truly knows or understands what humans have named it. But, of course, it does lend itself to a good joke or two. For example, why did the Danish Chicken Dog cross the road . . .

Madeline: What is the difference between a hippopotamus and a Chihuahua?
Pedro: About 2,200 pounds (999 kilograms)!

Jacob: What do you call twelve Chihuahuas?
Phillip: A dozen!

Tali: Why do Chihuahuas have such short necks?
Jenna: Because their heads are so close to their bodies!

Mara: What did the elephant say when it saw the Chihuahuas coming down the road?
Marina: Look out for the mice!

From the "Grim Tails" department: You've probably heard of a billy goat or heard the folktale of the Three Billy Goats Gruff. *But, have you heard of the Billy dog? The Billy is a hunting dog that hails from France and was originally used to track wild boars and deer.*

Henry: What did the tangerine say when it saw the Chihuahua?
Mo: Nothing. Tangerines can't talk!

Is it possible to have a joke book about dogs
and not mention cats?
— No!